LAB HAND BOOK OF COMPILER DESIGN

COMPILER

JAI PRATAP DIXIT

DEDICATED TO AMBALIKA INSTITUTE OF MANAGEMENT AND TECHNOLOGY

Contents

Preface *vii*

1. Chapter 1 1
2. Chapter 2 5
3. Chapter 3 8
4. Chapter 4 13
5. Chapter 5 19
6. Chapter 6 23
7. Chapter 7 25
8. Chapter 8 28
9. Chapter 9 32
10. Chapter 10 33
11. Chapter 11 36

Preface

Compiler is a software which takes as input a program written in a High-Level language and translates it into its equivalent program in Low Level program. Compilers teaches us how real-world applications are working and how to design them. Learning Compilers gives us with both theoretical and practical knowledge that is crucial in order to implement a programming language. It gives you a new level of understanding of a language in order to make better use of the language (optimization is just one example). Sometimes just using a compiler is not enough. You need to optimize the compiler itself for your application. Compilers have a general structure that can be applied in many other applications, from debuggers to simulators to 3D applications to a browser and even a cmd / shell. understanding compilers and how they work makes it super simple to understand all the rest. a bit like a deep understanding of math will help you to understand geometry or physics. We cannot do physics without the math. not on the same level. Just using something (read: tool, device, software, programming language) is usually enough when everything goes as expected. But if something goes wrong, only a true understanding of the inner workings and details will help to fix it. Even more specifically, Compilers are super elaborated / sophisticated systems (architecturally speaking). If you will say that can or have written a compiler by yourself - there will be no doubt as to your capabilities as a programmer. There is nothing you cannot do in the Software realm. So, better be a pilot who have the knowledge and mechanics of an airplane than the one who just know how to fly. Every computer scientist can do much better if have knowledge of compilers apart from the domain and technical knowledge. Compiler design lab provides deep understanding of how programming language Syntax, Semantics are used in translation into machine equivalents apart from the knowledge of various compiler generation tools like LEX,YACC etc.

CHAPTER ONE

PRACTICAL-1

Implementation of LEXICAL ANALYZER for IF STATEMENT

```
#include<stdio.h>
#include<ctype.h>
#include<conio.h>
#include<string.h>
char vars[100][100];
int vcnt;
char input[1000],c;
char token[50],tlen;int state=0,pos=0,i=0,id;
char*getAddress(char str[])
{
for(i=0;i<vcnt;i++)if(strcmp(str,vars[i])==0)return
vars[i];
strcpy(vars[vcnt],str);return vars[vcnt++];
}
intisrelop(char c){if(c=='>'||c=='<'||c=='|'||c=='=')return
1;
elsereturn 0;
}
int main(void)
{
clrscr();
printf("Enter the Input String:");
```

```
gets(input);
do{c=input[pos];
putchar(c);
switch(state){case 0:if(c=='i')state=1;
break;
case 1:
if(c=='f')
{printf("\t<1,1>\n");
state =2
;
}
break;
case2:
if(isspace(c))printf("\b");
if(isalpha(c))
{
token[0]=c;
tlen=1;
state=3;
}
if(isdigit(c))state=4;
if(isrelop(c))state=5;
if(c==';')printf("\t<4,4>\n");
if(c=='(')printf("\t<5,0>\n");if(c==')')
printf("\t<5,1>\n");
if(c=='{') printf("\t<6,1>\n");
if(c=='}')
printf("\t<6,2>\n");
break;
case 3:
if(!isalnum(c)){token[tlen]='\o';
printf("\b\t<2,%p>\n",getAddress(token));
state=2;
```

```
pos--;
}
else token[tlen++]=c;
break;
case 4:
if(!isdigit(c))
{
printf("\b\t<3,%p>\n",&input[pos]);
state=2;
pos--;
}
break;
case 5:
id=input[pos-1];
if(c=='=')
printf("\t<%d,%d>\n",id*10,id*10);
else
{
printf("\b\t<%d,%d>\n",id,id);
pos--;
}
state=2;
break;
}
pos++;
}
while(c!=0);
getch();
return 0;
}
```

OUTPUT

```
Enter the input string: if(a>=b) max=a;\
                        If <1,1>
```

(<5,0>

A <2,0960>

>= <620,620>

B <2,09c4>

) <5,1>

Max <2,0A28>

= <61,61>

A <2,0A8c>

; <4,4>

CHAPTER TWO

PRACTICAL-2

Implementation of LEXICAL ANALYZER for ARITHMETIC EXPRESSION

```
#include<stdio.h>
#include<ctype.h>
#include<conio.h>
#include<string.h>
char vars[100][100];
int vcnt;char input[1000],c;
char token[50],tlen;
int state=0,pos=0,i=0,id;
char *getAddress(char str[])
{
for(i=0;i<vcnt;i++)
if(strcmp(str,vars[i])==0)return vars[i];
strcpy(vars[vcnt],str);
return vars[vcnt++];
}
intisrelop(char c)
{
if(c=='+'||c=='-'||c=='*'||c=='/'||c=='%'||c=='^')
return 1;
else
return 0;
}
```

```
int main(void)
{
clrscr();
printf("Enter the Input String:");
gets(input);
do
{
c=input[pos];
putchar(c);
switch(state){case
0:if(isspace(c))printf("\b");if(isalpha(c)){token[0]=c;
tlen=1;
state=1;
}
if(isdigit(c))
state=2;
if(isrelop(c))state=3;if(c==';')printf("\t<3,3>\n");
if(c=='=') printf("\t<4,4>\n");
break;case 1: if(!isalnum(c))
{
token[tlen]='\o';
printf("\b\t<1,%p>\n",getAddress(token));
state=0;
pos--;
}
else token[tlen++]=c;
break;
case 2:
if(!isdigit(c))
{
printf("\b\t<2,%p>\n",&input[pos]);
state=0;
pos--;
```

```
}
break;
case 3:
id=input[pos-1];
if(c=='=')
printf("\t<%d,%d>\n",id*10,id*10);else{printf("\b\
t<%d,%d>\n",id,id);pos--;
}
state=0;
break;
}
pos++;
}
while(c!=0);
getch();
return 0;
}
```

OUTPUT

```
Enter the Input String: a=a*2+b/c; a <1,08CE>
= <4,4>
A <1,08CE>
* <42,42>
2 <2,04E9>
+ <43,43>
B <1,0932>
/ <47,47>
C <1,0996>
; <3,3>
```

CHAPTER THREE

PRACTICAL-3

Construction of NFA from REGULAR EXPRESSION

```
#include <stdio.h>
#include <stdlib.h>
#include <string.h>
#include <stdbool.h>
#include <math.h>
int row = 0;
struct node{
int data;
struct node* next;
char edgetype;
}typedef node;
// Adds an edge to an adjacency list
node* push(node* first , char edgetype , int data){
node* new_node = (node*)malloc(sizeof(node));
new_node->edgetype = edgetype;
new_node->data = data;
new_node->next = NULL;
if (first==NULL){
first = new_node;
return new_node;
}
first->next = push(first->next,edgetype,data);
return first;
```

```
}
//Recursive function to check acceptance of input
int nfa(node** graph, int current, char* input,
int* accept, int start){
if (start==(int)strlen(input))
return accept[current];
node* temp = graph[current];
while (temp != NULL){
if (input[start]==temp->edgetype) {
if (nfa(graph,temp->data,input,accept,start+1==1)){
return 1;
}
}
temp=temp->next;
}
return 0;
}
//Function to generate binary strings of size n
void generate(char** arr, int size, char *a){
if (size==0){
strcpy(arr[row], a);
row++;
return;
}
char b0[20] = {'\0'};
char b1[20] = {'\0'};
b0[0] = '0';
b1[0] = '1';
generate((char**)arr, size-1, strcat(b0,a)); //Add 0 in
front
generate((char**)arr, size-1, strcat(b1,a)); //Add 1 in
front
return;
```

```
}
int main(){
int n;
int i, j;
scanf("%d", &n); //Number of nodes
node* graph[n+1]; //Create a graph
for (i=0;i<n+1;i++)
graph[i]=NULL;
int accept[n+1]; //Array to store state of vertex
for (i=0; i<n; i++){
//Index of vertex , Acceptance state , Number of edges
int index,acc,number_nodes;
scanf("%d%d%d",&index,&acc,&number_nodes);
accept[index]=acc; //Store acceptance
for (j=0;j<number_nodes;j++) //Add all edges{
int node_add;
int edge;
scanf("%d%d",&edge,&node_add);
graph[index] = push(graph[index],'0'+edge,node_add);
}
}
int size = 1; //Size of input
int count = 0; //Keep count of output strings
if (accept[1]==1) //Check for empty string{
printf("e\n");
count++;
}
while (count < 11){
char** arr;
int power = pow(2,size);
arr = (char**)malloc(power*sizeof(char*));
for (i=0;i<power;i++)
arr[i] = (char*)malloc(size*sizeof(char));
```

```
char a[20] = {'\0'};
generate((char**)arr,size,a); //Generate inputs
for (i=0; i<power; i++){
char input[20] = {'\0'};
for (j=0; j<size; j++){
char foo[2];
foo[0] = arr[i][size-1-j];
foo[1] = '\0';
strcat(input,foo);
//Copy generated string input
}
int result = nfa(graph,1,input,accept,0);
// Store result of nfa
if (result==1){
printf("%s\n",input);
count++;
}
if (count==10)
return 0;
}
size++; //Increment size of binary string input
row=0;
}
return 0;
}
```

OUTPUT

Input

4

1 0 4 0 1 0 2 1 1 1 3

2 0 1 0 4

3 0 1 1 4

4 1 2 0 4 1 4

Output

```
00
    11
    000
    001
    011
```

CHAPTER FOUR

PRACTICAL-4

Construction of DFA from NFA

```
#include<iostream.h>
#include<string.h>
#include<stdio.h>
#include<conio.h>
#include<stdlib.h>
char nfa[50][50],s[20],st[10][20],eclos[20],input[20];
int x,e,top=0,topd=0,n=0,ns,nos,in;
int checke(char a)
{
int i;
for(i=0;i<e;i++)
{
if(eclos[i]==a)
return i;
}
return -1;
}
int check(char a)
{
int i;
for(i=0;i<in;i++)
{
if(input[i]==a)
```

```
return i;
}
return -1;
}
void push(char a)
{
s[top]=a;
top++;
}
char pop()
{
top--;
return s[top];
}
void pushd(char *a)
{
strcpy(st[topd],a);
topd++;
}

char *popd()
{
topd--;
return st[topd];
}
int ctoi(char a)
{
int i=a-48;
return i;
}
char itoc(int a)
{
char i=a+48;
```

```
return i;
}
char *eclosure(char *a)
{
int i,j;
char c;
for(i=0;i<strlen(a);i++)
push(a[i]);
e=strlen(a);
strcpy(eclos,a);
while(top!=0)
{
c=pop();
for(j=0;j<ns;j++)
{
if(nfa[ctoi(c)][j]=='e')
{
if(check(itoc(j))==-1)
{
eclos[e]=itoc(j);
push(eclos[e]);
e++;
}
}
}
}
eclos[e]='\0';
return eclos;
}

void main()
{
int i,j,k,count;
```

```
char ec[20],a[20],b[20],c[20],dstates[10][10];
clrscr();
cout<<"Enter the number of states"<<endl;
cin>>ns;
for(i=0;i<ns;i++)
{
for(j=0;j<ns;j++)
{
cout<<"Move["<<i<<"]["<<j<<"]";
cin>>nfa[i][j];
if(nfa[i][j]!='-'&&nfa[i][j]!='e')
{
if((check(nfa[i][j]))==-1)
input[in++]=nfa[i][j];
}
}
}
topd=0;
nos=0;
c[0]=itoc(0);
c[1]='\0';
pushd(eclosure(c));
strcpy(dstates[nos],eclosure(c));
for(x=0;x<in;x++)
cout<<"\t"<<input[x];
cout<<"\n";
while(topd>0)
{
strcpy(a,popd());
cout<<a<<"\t";
for(i=0;i<in;i++)
{
int len=0;
```

```
for(j=0;j<strlen(a);j++)
{
int x=ctoi(a[j]);
for(k=0;k<ns;k++)
{
if(nfa[x][k]==input[i])
ec[len++]=itoc(k);
}
}
ec[len]='\0';
strcpy(b,eclosure(ec));
count=0;
for(j=0;j<=nos;j++)
{
if(strcmp(dstates[j],b)==0)
count++;
}
if(count==0)
{
if(b[0]!='\0')
{
nos++;
pushd(b);
strcpy(dstates[nos],b);
}
}
cout<<b<<"\t";
}
cout<<endl;
}
getch();
}
```

OUTPUT

Enter the number of states

5

Move[0][0]-

Move[0][1]e

Move[0][2]-

Move[0][3]e

Move[0][4]-

Move[1][0]-

Move[1][1]-

Move[1][2]a

Move[1][3]-

Move[1][4]-

Move[2][0]-

Move[2][1]e

Move[2][2]-

Move[2][3]e

Move[2][4]-

Move[3][0]-

Move[3][1]-

Move[3][2]-

Move[3][3]-

Move[3][4]b

Move[4][0]-

Move[4][1]-

Move[4][2]-

Move[4][3]-

Move[4][4]-

a b

013 213 4

4

213 213 4

CHAPTER FIVE

PRACTICAL-5

Implementation of SHIFT REDUCE PARSING ALGORITHM

```
#include<stdio.h>
#include<stdlib.h>
#include<string.h>
//Global Variables
int z = 0, i = 0, j = 0, c = 0;
// Modify array size to increase
// length of string to be parsed
char a[16], ac[20], stk[15], act[10];
// This Function will check whether
// the stack contain a production rule
// which is to be Reduce.
// Rules can be E->2E2 , E->3E3 , E->4
void check()
{
// Copying string to be printed as action
strcpy(ac,"REDUCE TO E -> ");
// c=length of input string
for(z = 0; z < c; z++)
{
//checking for producing rule E->4
if(stk[z] == '4')
{
```

```
printf("%s4", ac);
stk[z] = 'E';
stk[z + 1] = '\0';
//printing action
printf("\n$%s\t%s$\t", stk, a);
}
}
for(z = 0; z < c - 2; z++)
{
//checking for another production
if(stk[z] == '2' && stk[z + 1] == 'E' &&
stk[z + 2] == '2')
{ printf("%s2E2", ac);
stk[z] = 'E';
stk[z + 1] = '\0';
stk[z + 2] = '\0';
printf("\n$%s\t%s$\t", stk, a);
i = i - 2;
}
}
for(z=0; z<c-2; z++)
{
//checking for E->3E3
if(stk[z] == '3' && stk[z + 1] == 'E' &&
stk[z + 2] == '3')
{
printf("%s3E3", ac);
stk[z]='E';
stk[z + 1]='\0';
stk[z + 1]='\0';
printf("\n$%s\t%s$\t", stk, a);
i = i - 2;
}
```

```
}
return ; //return to main
}
//Driver Function
int main()
{
printf("GRAMMAR is -\nE->2E2 \nE->3E3 \nE->4\n");
// a is input string
strcpy(a,"32423");
// strlen(a) will return the length of a to c
c=strlen(a);
// "SHIFT" is copied to act to be printed
strcpy(act,"SHIFT");
// This will print Labels (column name)
printf("\nstack \t input \t action");
// This will print the initial
// values of stack and input
printf("\n$\t%s$\t", a);
// This will Run upto length of input string
for(i = 0; j < c; i++, j++)
{
// Printing action
printf("%s", act);
// Pushing into stack
stk[i] = a[j];
stk[i + 1] = '\0';
// Moving the pointer
a[j]=' ';
// Printing action
printf("\n$%s\t%s$\t", stk, a);
// Call check function ..which will
// check the stack whether its contain
// any production or not
```

```
check();
}
// Rechecking last time if contain
// any valid production then it will
// replace otherwise invalid
check();
// if top of the stack is E(starting symbol)
// then it will accept the input
if(stk[0] == 'E' && stk[1] == '\0')
printf("Accept\n");
else //else reject
printf("Reject\n");
}
```

OUTPUT

Output –

GRAMMAR is -

E->2E2

E->3E3

E->4

stack input action

$ 32423$ SHIFT

$3 2423$ SHIFT

$32 423$ SHIFT

$324 23$ REDUCE TO E -> 4

$32E 23$ SHIFT

$32E2 3$ REDUCE TO E -> 2E2

$3E 3$ SHIFT

$3E3 $ REDUCE TO E -> 3E3

$E $ Accept

CHAPTER SIX

PRACTICAL-6

Implementation of OPERATOR PRECEDENCE PARSER

```
#include<stdlib.h>
#include<stdio.h>
#include<string.h>
// function f to exit from the loop
// if given condition is not true
void f()
{
printf("Not operator grammar");
exit(0);
}
void main()
{
char grm[20][20], c;
// Here using flag variable,
// considering grammar is not operator grammar
int i, n, j = 2, flag = 0;
// taking number of productions from user
scanf("%d", &n);
for (i = 0; i < n; i++)
scanf("%s", grm[i]);
for (i = 0; i < n; i++) {
c = grm[i][2];
while (c != '\0') {
```

```
if (grm[i][3] == '+' || grm[i][3] == '-'
|| grm[i][3] == '*' || grm[i][3] == '/')
flag = 1;
else {
flag = 0;
f();
}
if (c == '$') {
flag = 0;
f();
}
c = grm[i][++j];
}
}
if (flag == 1)
printf("Operator grammar");
}
```

OUTPUT

Input :3

A=A*A

B=AA

A=$

Output : Not operator grammar

Input :2

A=A/A

B=A+A

Output : Operator grammar

CHAPTER SEVEN

PRACTICAL-7

Implementation of RECURSIVE DESCENT PARSER

```
#include<stdio.h>
#include<string.h>
#include<ctype.h>

char input[10];
int i,error;
void E();
void T();
void Eprime();
void Tprime();
void F();
main()
{
i=0;
error=0;
printf("Enter an arithmetic expression : "); // Eg: a+a*a
gets(input);
E();
if(strlen(input)==i&&error==0)
printf("\nAccepted..!!!\n");
else printf("\nRejected..!!!\n");
}
void E()
```

```
{
T();
Eprime();
}
void Eprime()
{
if(input[i]=='+')
{
i++;
T();
Eprime();
}
}
void T()
{
F();
Tprime();
}
void Tprime()
{
if(input[i]=='*')
{
i++;
F();
Tprime();
}
}
void F()
{
if(isalnum(input[i]))i++;
else if(input[i]=='(')
{
i++;
```

```
E();
if(input[i]==')')
i++;

else error=1;
}

else error=1;
}
```

OUTPUT

a+(a*a) a+a*a , (a), a , a+a+a*a+a.... etc are accepted ++a, a***a, +a, a*, ((a . . . etc are rejected.

CHAPTER EIGHT

PRACTICAL-8

Implementation of CODE OPTIMIZATION TECHNIQUES

```
#include<stdio.h>
#include<conio.h>
#include<string.h>
struct op
{ char l;
char r[20];
}
op[10],pr[10];
void main()
{ int a,i,k,j,n,z=0,m,q;
char *p,*l;
char temp,t;
char *tem;
clrscr();
printf("Enter the Number of Values:");
scanf("%d",&n);
for(i=0;i<n;i++)
{
printf("left: ");
op[i].l=getche();
printf("\tright: ");
scanf("%s",op[i].r);
```

```
}
printf("Intermediate Code\n") ;
for(i=0;i<n;i++)
{
printf("%c=",op[i].l);
printf("%s\n",op[i].r);
}
for(i=0;i<n-1;i++)
{ temp=op[i].l;
for(j=0;j<n;j++)
{
p=strchr(op[j].r,temp);
if(p)
{
pr[z].l=op[i].l;
strcpy(pr[z].r,op[i].r);
z++; }}}
pr[z].l=op[n-1].l;
strcpy(pr[z].r,op[n-1].r);
z++;
printf("nAfter Dead Code Eliminationn");
for(k=0;k<z;k++) {
printf("%ct=",pr[k].l);
printf("%sn",pr[k].r);
}
for(m=0;m<z;m++) {
tem=pr[m].r;
for(j=m+1;j<z;j++) {
p=strstr(tem,pr[j].r);
if(p) {
t=pr[j].l;
pr[j].l=pr[m].l;
for(i=0;i<z;i++) {
```

```
l=strchr(pr[i].r,t) ;
if(l) {
a=l-pr[i].r;
printf("pos: %d",a);
pr[i].r[a]=pr[m].l; }}}}}
printf("Eliminate Common Expression\n");
for(i=0;i<z;i++)
{
printf("%c\t=",pr[i].l);
printf("%s\n",pr[i].r);
}
for(i=0;i<z;i++)
{
for(j=i+1;j<z;j++)
{
q=strcmp(pr[i].r,pr[j].r);
if((pr[i].l==pr[j].l)&&!q)
{
pr[i].l='\0';
strcpy(pr[i].r,'\0');
}}}
printf("Optimized Code\n");
for(i=0;i<z;i++)
{ if(pr[i].l!='\0')
{
printf("%c=",pr[i].l);
printf("%s\n",pr[i].r);
}
}
getch();
}
```

OUTPUT

INPUT & OUTPUT:

Enter the Number of Values:5
left: a right: 9
left: b right: c+d
left: e right: c+d
left: f right: b+e
left: r right: f
Intermediate Code
a=9
b=c+d
e=c+d
f=b+e
r=f
nAfter Dead Code Eliminationnbt=c+dnet=c+dnft=b+enrt=fnpos: 2Eliminate Common Expression
b =c+d
b =c+d
f =b+b
r =f
Optimized Code
b=c+d
f=b+b

CHAPTER NINE

CHAPTER TEN

PRACTICAL-9

Implementation of CODE GENERATOR

Program:

```
#include<stdio.h>
#include<conio.h>
#include<string.h>
char op[2],arg1[5],arg2[5],result[5];
void main()
{
FILE *fp1,*fp2;
fp1=fopen("input.txt","r");
fp2=fopen("output.txt","w");
while(!feof(fp1))
{

fscanf(fp1,"%s%s%s%s",op,arg1,arg2,result);
if(strcmp(op,"+")==0)
{
fprintf(fp2,"\nMOV R0,%s",arg1);
fprintf(fp2,"\nADD R0,%s",arg2);
fprintf(fp2,"\nMOV %s,R0",result);
}
if(strcmp(op,"*")==0)
{
fprintf(fp2,"\nMOV R0,%s",arg1);
```

```
fprintf(fp2,"\nMUL R0,%s",arg2);
fprintf(fp2,"\nMOV %s,R0",result);
}
if(strcmp(op,"-")==0)
{
fprintf(fp2,"\nMOV R0,%s",arg1);
fprintf(fp2,"\nSUB R0,%s",arg2);
fprintf(fp2,"\nMOV %s,R0",result);
}
if(strcmp(op,"/")==0)
{
fprintf(fp2,"\nMOV R0,%s",arg1);
fprintf(fp2,"\nDIV R0,%s",arg2);
fprintf(fp2,"\nMOV %s,R0",result);
}
if(strcmp(op,"=")==0)
{
fprintf(fp2,"\nMOV R0,%s",arg1);
fprintf(fp2,"\nMOV %s,R0",result);
}
}
fclose(fp1);
fclose(fp2);
getch();
}
}
```

OUTPUT

input.txt

```
+ a b t1
* c d t2
- t1 t2 t
= t ? x
```

output.txt

```
MOV R0,a
ADD R0,b
MOV t1,R0
MOV R0,c
MUL R0,d
MOV t2,R0
MOV R0,t1
SUB R0,t2
MOV t,R0
MOV R0,t
MOV x,R0
```

CHAPTER ELEVEN

VIVA QUESTIONS

a. **What is lexical analyzer?**
b. **Which compiler is used for lexical analysis?**
c. **What is the output of Lexical analyzer?**
d. **Which Finite state machines are used in lexical analyzer design?**
e. **What is the role of regular expressions, grammars in Lexical Analizer?**
f. **What is are the functions of a Scanner?**
g. **What is Token?**
h. **What is lexeme, Pattern?**
a. **What is purpose of Lex?**
j. **What are the other tools used in Lexical Analysis?**
k. **What is a parser and state the Role of it?**
ax. **Types of parsers? Examples to each**
all. **What are the Tools available for implementation?**
n. **How do you calculate FIRST(),FOLLOW() sets used in Parsing Table construction?**
o. **What is yacc? Are there any other tools avilable for parser generation?**
p. **How do you use it?**
q. **Structure of parser specification program**

What is abstract syntax tree?

9 798887 724676

Printed by Libri Plureos GmbH in Hamburg,
Germany